SACRAMENTO PUBLIC LIBRARY
828 "I" Street
Sacramento, CA 95814

D0787609

How I Feel

I Feel Worried

By Connor Stratton

www.littlebluehousebooks.com

Copyright © 2021 by Little Blue House, Mendota Heights, MN 55120. All rights reserved. No part of this book may be reproduced or utilized in any form or by any means without written permission from the publisher.

Little Blue House is distributed by North Star Editions:
sales@northstareditions.com | 888-417-0195

Produced for Little Blue House by Red Line Editorial.

Photographs ©: Shutterstock Images, cover, 4, 6–7, 10–11, 16–17, 18 (top), 18 (bottom), 20–21, 24 (top left), 24 (top right), 24 (bottom left); iStockphoto, 9, 12 (top), 12 (bottom), 15, 23, 24 (bottom right)

Library of Congress Control Number: 2020913848

ISBN
978-1-64619-300-4 (hardcover)
978-1-64619-318-9 (paperback)
978-1-64619-354-7 (ebook pdf)
978-1-64619-336-3 (hosted ebook)

Printed in the United States of America
Mankato, MN
012021

About the Author

Connor Stratton enjoys writing books for children and watching movies, such as *Inside Out*. He's always trying to understand his feelings better. He lives in Minnesota.

Table of Contents

Why I'm Worried 5

How It Feels 13

Feeling Better 19

Glossary 24

Index 24

Why I'm Worried

Sometimes I feel worried. I worry about going to school because I won't be with my parents.

I worry about going to the doctor.
Getting a shot is scary because it might hurt.

doctor
shot

Sometimes I go to a
new camp.
I don't know anyone there.
I worry I won't
make friends.

I worry about my parents. Sometimes they look sad or angry, and I worry I did something wrong.

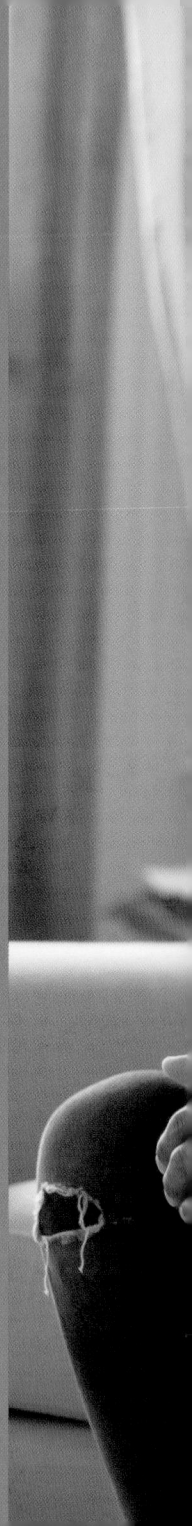

parents

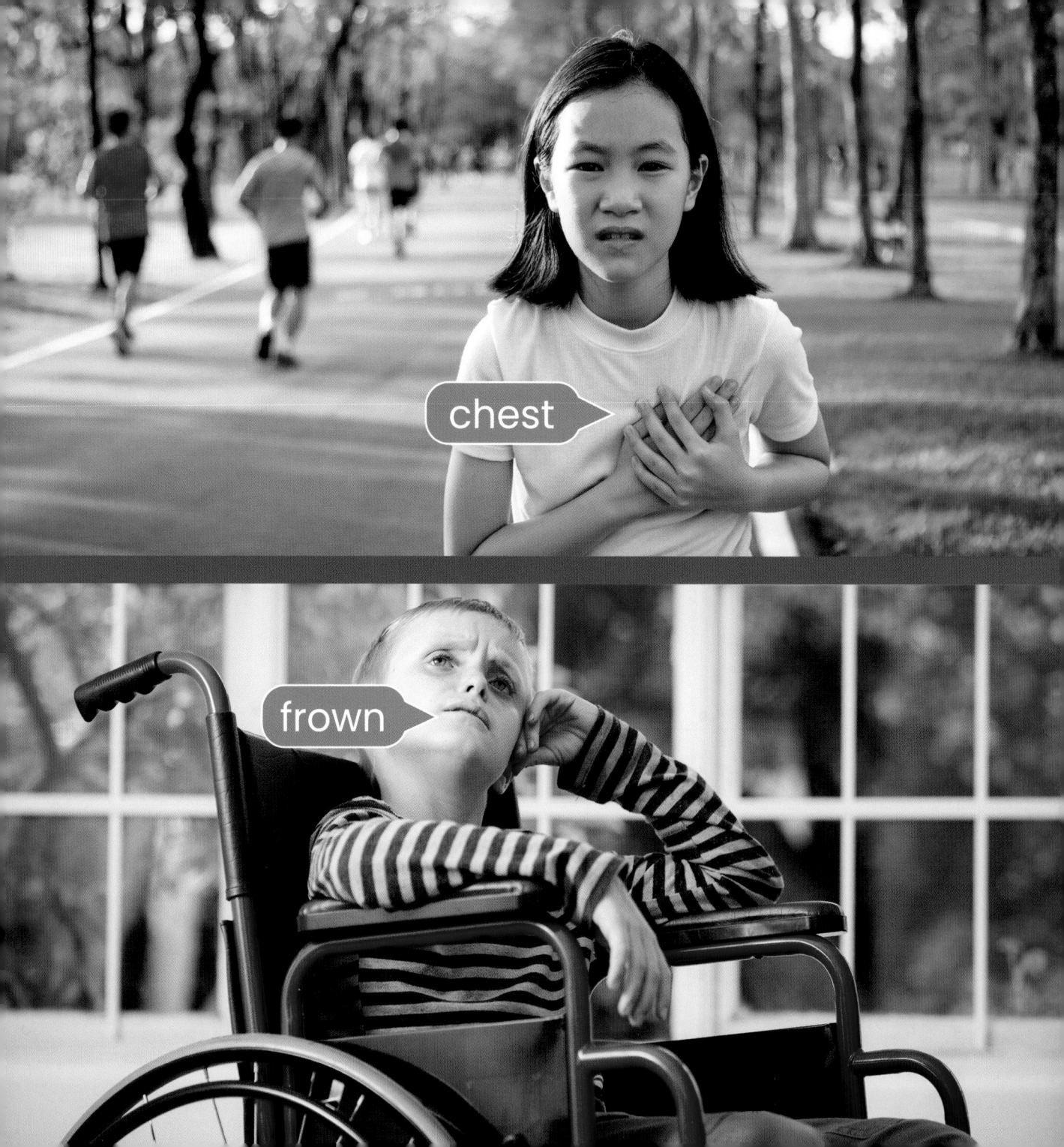
chest
frown

How It Feels

When I feel worried, my chest starts to hurt. Sometimes I frown too.

I have lots of thoughts
when I'm worried.
I think about something
bad that could happen.

Sometimes I feel
really worried.
Then it is hard to breathe.

dad
teacher

Feeling Better

I talk to people when I
feel worried.
Sometimes I talk to my dad.
Sometimes I talk to
my teacher.

I tell my mom why
I'm worried.
She tells me feeling
worried is okay.
But I don't need to worry.

mom

My dad gives me a hug
and holds me tight.
I don't feel
worried anymore.

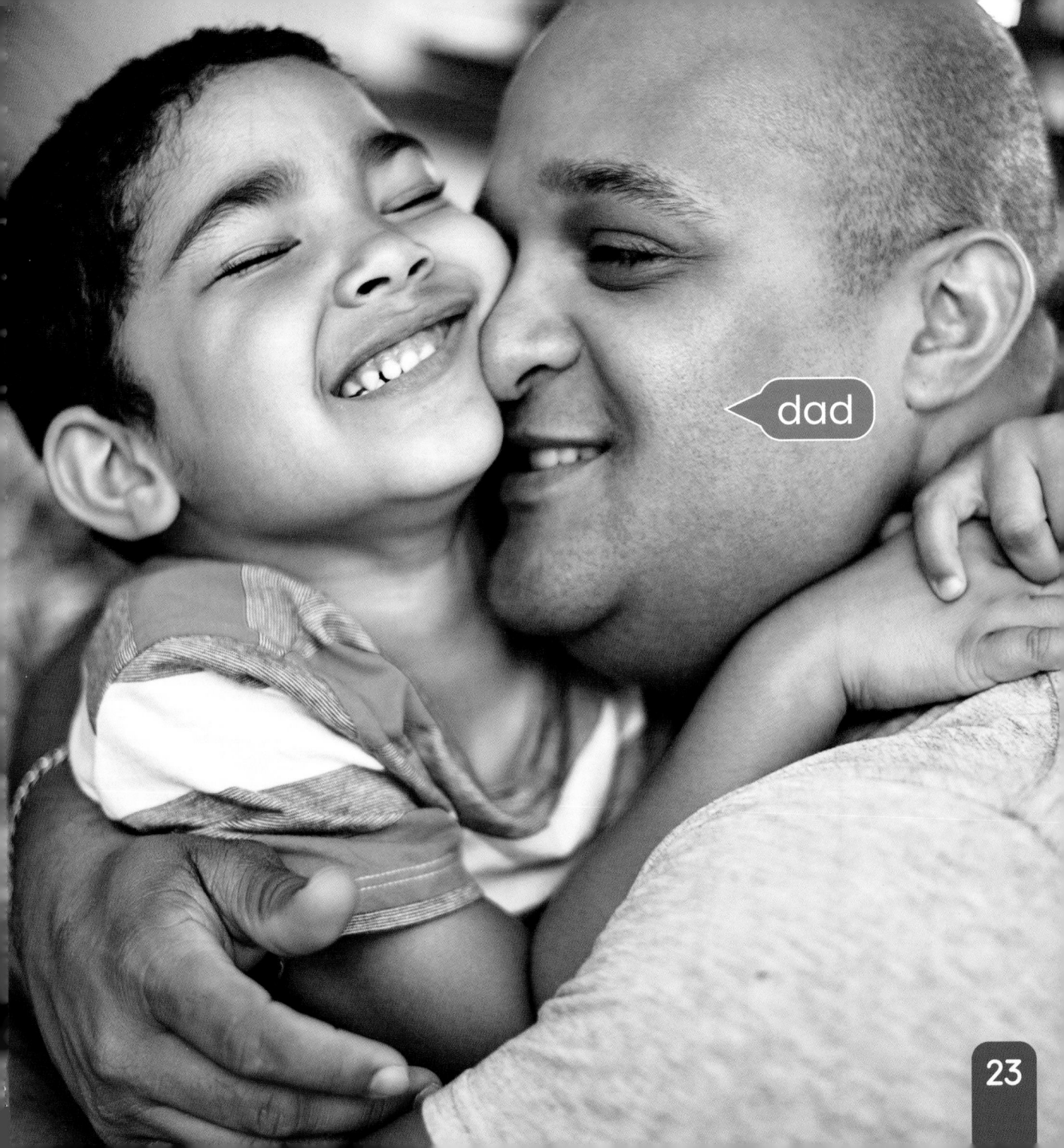
dad

Glossary

dad

mom

frown

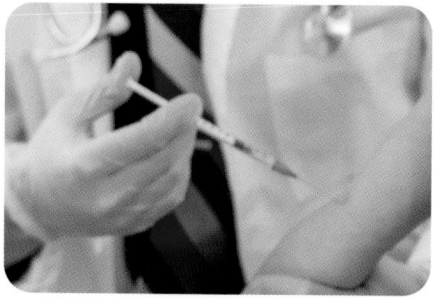

shot

Index

C
camp, 8

H
hug, 22

S
school, 5

T
teacher, 19